PAPER BAGS/ PLASTIC BAGS

UNCLOG SHOWERHEADS

and Other Simple Solutions

Betsy Rossen Elliot

Contents

Housecleaning and Housekeeping

You long to create and maintain a clean, orderly home, but you lack the time, energy, help, cleaning concoctions, equipment, know-how, or money to reach the goal.

Never fear! A regiment of professionals—plastic and paper household products, that is—has been cross-trained in the household arts. Among those available for duty: a plastic bag that unclogs a showerhead, a paper bag that's not too proud to clean a teddy bear, and a paper plate that stoops to act as a dustpan in times of need.

BATTLE OF THE BATHROOM

♦ If you have a clogged showerhead that is too stubborn to come apart, make a soaking bag for it by filling a GLAD Food Storage Bag with Heinz Distilled White Vinegar. Wrap the filled bag around the showerhead and attach it with a rubber band. Let it sit overnight, and by morning the showerhead should come loose (even if it doesn't, the clog should be gone because any mineral deposits should be dissolved).

- Make easy work of cleaning a porcelain sink. Make a solution of equal parts Clorox Regular-Bleach and water. (Be sure to wear rubber gloves.) Cover the surface of the sink with a thick layer of Scott Towels, then saturate them with the solution. Remove the towels after 5 minutes; rinse with clear water.

- When soap scum, rust, or other stains just won't come off a white porcelain tub with average scrubbing (a common problem with older and antique tubs), add enough water to 20 Mule Team Borax to make a paste. Make sure it's sticky enough to adhere to the sides of the tub. Apply the paste onto stubborn stains using a paintbrush, then cover with damp Scott Towels. Let sit 1 hour, then scrub with a nylon dish scrubber or a scrubbing brush. Thoroughly rinse tub with warm water.

ASSIGNMENT: KITCHEN

- Use chalk to clean polished marble and metal surfaces. Crush white Crayola chalk in a GLAD Food Storage Zipper Bag, tapping it gently with a hammer. Dip a soft cloth into the powder and rub.

- Trying to vacuum under the refrigerator or another hard-to-reach spot? Put a cardboard tube from a roll of Scott Towels, gift wrap, or another product on the end of the hose attachment. For any narrow

Roll of History

openings, bend or flatten the tube.

◆ Clearing the table after a big dinner party can be a challenge. To get a head start on doing the dishes, line a large bowl with a plastic grocery bag, handles overlapping the edges. Place it prominently in your kitchen with a rubber spatula alongside. As the plates are brought into the kitchen, scrape the scraps right into the bowl. Once the plates are clean, it's a snap to pick the bag up by the handles and toss.

◆ Loosen burned-on food from a barbecue grill rack by placing the rack in a GLAD trash bag. Mix 1 cup ARM & HAMMER Baking Soda and ½ cup Parsons' Ammonia and pour over rack. Close the bag; let it sit overnight. Scrub and rinse well in the morning. Be sure to wear rubber gloves; use ammonia only in a well-ventilated area.

ALL AROUND THE ABODE
Floors and Walls

- When chewing gum is stuck in a carpet or rug, put a few ice cubes in a GLAD Food Storage Zipper Bag and place it directly on the gum. When gum hardens, use a dull knife to scrape it off.

- This same method works on chewing gum stuck to a hardwood floor—set a GLAD Food Storage Zipper Bag of ice cubes on top of the gum. After gum hardens, use an old credit card to pry it loose. If necessary, polish that area of the floor after gum is removed.

- Candle wax has spilled on your carpeting. Before it hardens, lay a brown paper bag or a thick layer of Scott Towels over the wax and apply an iron on a medium setting (no steam). If necessary, repeat with a fresh spot of paper. Much, if not all, of the wax should be absorbed.

- Remove the dust from a dust mop with the assistance of a large paper bag. Place the bag over the mop head; secure it with a rubber band. Vigorously shake the mop by the handle. Lay the mop on its side for several minutes to allow the dust to settle. Carefully open the bag and remove the mop; dispose of the bag properly.

- Take a grease spot off wallpaper by first blotting it with a Scott Towel, then lightly rubbing the spot using a damp cloth sprinkled with Argo Corn Starch. Once the spot is gone, vacuum the area using an upholstery brush attachment.

- If you've misplaced your dustpan, use a Dixie paper plate instead. Cut it in half, moisten the edge a bit, and you have a new "pick-it-up"!

Decorating and Other Details

- Not sure where to hang a mirror or picture? Trace around it on a paper grocery or lunch bag, cut out the shape, and affix the shape to the wall with Scotch Masking Tape. When you've decided on the right spot—but before you remove the cutout—mark on the wall where the nail should go.

- Fine table linens are much easier to iron if you first place them in a GLAD Food Storage Zipper Bag and refrigerate for 6 to 24 hours.

- Plastic grocery bags can substitute for batting in pillows and valances.

- Try this trick for displaying flowers in a vase or other container that is not watertight: Fill a GLAD Freezer Zipper Bag about ⅓ full with water; place it in the container. Arrange cut flowers in the bag, zipping as needed to hold the stems in place.

- Clean artificial flowers using a paper grocery bag and Morton Salt. Pour ¼ cup salt into the bag, then add the flowers, blossom ends first. Close top and shake well. Carefully remove the flowers from the bag over a sink (or outside), then shake off the salt.

In and Out of Storage

- Fill a snack- or sandwich-size GLAD Food Storage Zipper Bag with potpourri. Seal it and poke several small holes to make an effective yet inexpensive sachet for your dresser drawers.

- Turn your closet into a cedar closet. Fill a large GLAD Food Storage Zipper Bag with cedar chips (available at pet stores for animal cages). Seal the bag and poke small holes all over both sides. Hang it in your closet.

- To clean musty items such as old postcards, magazines, sheet music, and books, place them in a paper bag with some Clabber Girl Baking Powder. Seal bag and change powder every few days until odor disappears.

KEEPING UP WITH KIDS

- Why spend money on an expensive store-bought drop cloth? Split open the seams of one or two GLAD trash bags; place on the floor under a high chair.

- Really smelly stuffed animals can be deodorized by placing them in a paper bag, adding ARM & HAMMER Baking Soda, and shaking vigorously. Store in bag overnight. Shake off the baking soda in the morning. If necessary, change the baking soda and repeat.

- Here's another method for cleaning stuffed animals or other cuddlies: Place a toy or a few small ones into a paper bag. Add some Argo Corn Starch to the bag, close tightly, and shake. Brush the corn starch off toys.

In the Kitchen

Paper bags, towels, and plates, as well as plastic bags and drinking straws, are familiar kitchen workers indeed. The delightful surprise is how these products can be employed in tasks other than the obvious.

Do any of the following scenarios sound at all familiar? Your guests will be served salad soon, but the lettuce isn't even washed yet. You're about to throw out yet another bag of stuck-together marshmallows. You promised to bring 6 dozen deviled eggs to the potluck supper but have limited time to make them. Time to panic? No, time for paper and plastic products.

HELP WITH THE PREP

- It's easiest to marinate meats not in a bowl or pan but in a quart- or gallon-size GLAD Food Storage Zipper Bag. The bag allows for full coverage, and you can easily flip the bag at intervals to make sure the marinade reaches all parts of the meat.

- When you need cracker crumbs for a recipe, put your crackers in a GLAD Food Storage Zipper Bag and squeeze out most of the air. Seal bag almost all the way, leaving it open at one corner so air can escape. Crush crackers by rolling a rolling pin up and down over the bag. This contains the mess, crushes the crackers, and keeps your rolling pin clean.

- To grease a pan or cookie sheet with Crisco All-Vegetable Shortening, slip a GLAD Food Storage Bag over your hand and dip it directly into the shortening container. Rub your hand over the pan to spread the shortening. Keep the bag in the shortening container for next time.

- Grind peppercorns or crush other whole spices by placing them in a snack-size GLAD Food Storage Zipper Bag and smashing with a meat-tenderizing hammer or even a rolling pin.

- If you try to soften a block of Kraft Philadelphia Cream Cheese in a microwave, you'll probably end up with a runny mess. Instead, remove the outer wrapping and seal the cream cheese in a pint-size GLAD Food Storage Zipper Bag. Place the bag in a bowl of hot water until the consistency is right.

- Dry lettuce faster than you can say "spin cycle"! Wash the leaves and shake off as much water as you can. Place them in a plastic grocery bag lined with Scott Towels. Grasp the bag by the handles (or let your kids have the fun) and whirl it around in circles until the lettuce is dry.

- Blot meats and vegetables dry with Scott Towels before cooking. They'll brown well instead of simply steaming.

- To revive wilted produce, sprinkle it with cool water, wrap it in a Scott Towel, and refrigerate for an hour.

- Picking silk from a freshly shucked ear of corn can be a tedious job. Speed up the process by wiping a damp Scott Towel across the ear; it will pick up the strands.

COOKING AND BAKING

- Mix and dispense in 2 easy steps—no cleanup required! Mix ingredients for deviled eggs or stuffed mushrooms by placing all ingredients in a GLAD Food Storage Zipper Bag. Seal it and knead to blend contents. To dispense the mixture, snip off a small corner of the still-sealed bag. Then just squeeze and stuff! When you're done, throw away your "dispenser."

- Melt chocolate without the messy bowl or pan to wash afterward. Pour chocolate chips, squares, or pieces into a GLAD Food Storage Zipper Bag and squeeze out most of the air. Seal and place bag in a pan of warm (but not boiling) water. When the chocolate is melted, snip off a small corner of the still-sealed bag; squeeze it into a recipe or use it to decorate a cake.

- Knead and roll out dough for a pie right inside a GLAD Food Storage Zipper Bag to create less mess.

- To make a simple cake-icing tool, put icing in a quart-size GLAD Freezer Zipper Bag. Squeeze the bag to make the icing go to one corner, then snip off a small piece of the bag at that corner. Twist and carefully squeeze the bag to make the icing come out. With practice, you'll be able to make designs and write names. (This trick also works for whipped cream.)

- Keep that cookbook clean while you cook. Open it to the proper page, then cover with or enclose it in a GLAD Food Storage Zipper Bag.

- What's the secret to perfectly round cookies? Cut an old Scott Towel tube lengthwise, open it, and line with GLAD Cling Wrap. Fill the tube with dough, evenly and completely; put the tube edges back together, then cover the whole roll with another layer of plastic wrap. Hold secure with rubber bands or tape. Refrigerate until ready to cut and bake.

No-Freeze Ice Cream

You don't need a fancy automatic ice-cream machine or an old-fashioned freezer to make ice cream in a hurry at home.

½ cup milk (whole, 2 percent, chocolate, or skim)
1 tablespoon Domino Sugar
¼ teaspoon McCormick Pure Vanilla Extract (or another flavoring)

Combine all ingredients in a sandwich-size GLAD Food Storage Zipper Bag. Zip the bag shut, then place it inside a quart- or gallon-size GLAD Food Storage Zipper Bag. Add enough ice to the outer bag to fill it halfway, then put in 6 tablespoons Morton Salt. Zip the larger bag shut. Now take turns tossing and turning, shaking and mixing the 2 bags in your hands. (It gets cold. You may want to hold a dishtowel while you do this if you don't have helpers.) After about 5 or 10 minutes of shaking, the mixture will be the consistency of ice cream.

Note: The ingredient amounts listed do not make very much ice cream, but don't double the recipe. If you need more, make several small batches.

THE FOOD STORAGE MYSTERY

Say Cheese!

◆ Prevent hard cheese from drying out by adding a few drops of Heinz Distilled White Vinegar to a Scott Towel moistened with water. Wrap the cheese in the paper towel and put it inside a GLAD Food Storage Zipper Bag.

◆ Extend the life of shredded cheese by storing it in the freezer. It will remain fresh and moisture-free longer. Store the cheese in its original bag, but put the bag inside a GLAD Freezer Zipper Bag.

Puzzling Produce

◆ Many fruits ripen more quickly and evenly at room temperature in a paper lunch bag. These include tomatoes, peaches, pears, and avocados. Wrap green bananas first in a damp dishtowel, then place in bag.

◆ Prolong the life of lettuce in your crisper drawer by wrapping it in a Scott Towel and enclosing in a GLAD Food Storage Zipper Bag before storing.

◆ Line your refrigerator's vegetable bin with Scott Towels to absorb moisture and fend off spoilage.

Sleuthing Out a Solution

◆ The marshmallows in your bag are stuck together? Add at least 1 teaspoon Argo Corn Starch to the bag, then hold it closed and shake. Once the excess moisture is absorbed, the marshmallows will come apart easily. Repackage any unused portion in a GLAD Freezer Zipper Bag and place in the freezer to keep fresh.

- Disgusting crud is hiding on and around the cutting wheel of your can opener. Get rid of it by closing the cutting wheel on the edge of a Scott Towel. Grip the handles together and turn the crank. The towel will wipe off the crud as the wheel cuts it.

MORE KITCHEN TIPS AND TRICKS

- Stacked pots and pans in a cabinet can get scratched. Line all but the top one with Scott Towels.

- Scott Towel cores make ideal sheaths in which to carry knives on picnics or camping trips. Flatten an unused tube, then close one end with Scotch Duct Tape. For smaller utensils, cut the tube into shorter pieces.

- When stacking china for storing, place a Dixie paper plate between each plate or saucer before putting them in a cupboard.

Gingerbread Kids

Here's a basic ginger-bread recipe with kid-size pans and kid-friendly instructions. It requires an adult cook, however.

In a Dixie cup, add 3 table-spoons packaged ginger-bread mix to 1 tablespoon water. Mix until moistened. Place the cup in the middle of an electric skillet; put its cover in place. Bake at 400°F. (Really. It won't burn!)

For a more advanced recipe, first mix the gingerbread as directed above. Then pour 1 teaspoon Crisco Pure Vegetable Oil into a second Dixie cup, sprinkle 1 teaspoon Domino Brown Sugar over the oil, and carefully add 1 tablespoon Dole Crushed Pineapple, drained, on top of the sugar. Pour your cup of gingerbread mix over the top and bake as directed above.

Feeling Good, Looking Good

When it comes to your family's grooming, hygiene, or health, you probably head for the hall closet, the bathroom vanity, or the medicine cabinet.

You may want to start turning to another room that contains the help you need: the kitchen. Check the kitchen drawers, cabinets, and pantry shelves for plastic zipper bags, paper and plastic grocery bags, paper towels, and more. Convenient and inexpensive, these products help you look your best even in the face of a cosmetic catastrophe; solve pressing problems concerning your ironing duties; remain calm though you've run out of baby wipes at a particularly inopportune time; or save the day when an ice pack is needed *right now.*

BEAUTY BOOSTS

◆ Store a few Q-tips cotton swabs and a small container of your favorite makeup remover in a snack- or sandwich-size GLAD Food Storage Zipper Bag. Carry it with you for emergency makeup fixes.

◆ Dip a few Q-tips cotton swabs in your favorite fragrance—whether perfume, cologne, or a scented oil—and carry them in your purse, sealed in a snack-size GLAD Food Storage Zipper Bag. Touch a swab to a few pressure points whenever you need a pick-me-up.

- Keep an emergency eye-relief kit in the freezer. Dampen Q-tips cotton swabs with water and store them in a small GLAD Freezer Zipper Bag in the freezer. To relieve tired eyes, roll a swab under each eye to reduce puffiness.

- Blow up a gallon-size GLAD Food Storage Zipper Bag for a handy bath pillow.

- To condition your hair naturally, apply ½ cup Kraft Mayonnaise to dry, unwashed hair. Carefully cover hair with a plastic grocery bag, being careful not to let it slip over your face, and leave on for 15 minutes. Wash as usual.

CARING FOR YOUR WARDROBE
Closets and Cleaning

- Construct a makeshift garment bag: Cut a hole in the center of the bottom seam of a GLAD trash bag (unscented, twist-tie variety). Turn it upside down and place over a hanger.

- If a good pair of pants has been on a regular hanger in the closet for a while, there's likely an obvious, ugly crease from the hanger. Next time, cut an old Scott Towel tube lengthwise and place it over the bottom of the hanger. (Cut the ends of the tube to shorten if necessary.) Tape the tube back together to make sure it doesn't fall off the hanger. Hang your pants

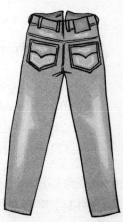

over the protective tube—good-bye, creases!

◆ When starch builds up on your iron, cut a piece from a brown paper grocery bag and sprinkle it with Morton Salt. Press the paper with the iron set on high heat (no steam).

◆ To remove a crease in knit fabrics, dip a clean cloth in a solution of 1 part Heinz Distilled White Vinegar and 2 parts water; apply to the crease. Place a brown paper bag over crease and iron area.

◆ Make your own fabric softener sheets by sprinkling Final Touch fabric softener on a Scott Towel, an O-Cel-O sponge, or a clean cloth and tossing it in the dryer.

Accessories

◆ Does your jewelry box look as if the chains have been wrestling? Solve that problem by dropping each chain through the end of a drinking straw that's been cut in half. Fasten the clasp on the outside of the straw.

◆ Insert Scott Towel cores into tall boots in storage to keep them from flopping over.

When the Rain Reigns

◆ Keep a GLAD trash bag in your car to provide a make-shift, if not stylish, rain poncho.

◆ What to do with a dripping umbrella, be it in the car or at an appointment? Once you're inside, fold it up and slip it in a newspaper delivery bag.

◆ Protect your shoes when you brave a muddy mess to pull weeds or take trash cans to the curb. Slip a pair of plastic grocery bags over your shoes and tie the handles at your ankles. Walk slowly and carefully to avoid slipping.

KID STUFF

◆ A group of GLAD Food Storage Zipper Bags makes an excellent organizer for carrying cotton balls, pacifiers, medicines, and the like inside a baby bag. Store each group of items in a sandwich-size bag, then place the smaller bags in a quart- or gallon-size bag.

◆ Carry a gallon-size GLAD Food Storage Zipper Bag in your purse or bag to use as a clean surface for emergency diaper changes.

◆ Make your own baby wipes for a fraction of the cost of store-bought. Mix 1 tablespoon Ivory Liquid Hand Cleanser (antibacterial), 1 teaspoon Johnson's Baby Oil, and ⅓ cup water. Fold several Scott Towels to fit inside a sandwich- or pint-size GLAD Food Storage Zipper

Bag. Pour enough of the mixture into the bag to get the towels damp, but not dripping. Seal the bag.

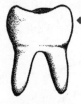 ◆ Go ahead... let your kids show off their first lost teeth. Just put them in a snack-size GLAD Food Storage Zipper Bag so they don't get misplaced.

◆ Help a child just learning to dress on his or her own by packing gallon-size GLAD Food Storage Zipper Bags with complete outfits, from shirts to socks. The child can pick a bag for the day, then dress all alone.

HYGIENE AND HEALTH HINTS

◆ Wish you could turn those slippery slivers of soap into something other than trash? Collect them in a sandwich-size GLAD Food Storage Zipper Bag. When the bag is about half full, place it in a pot of warm—but not boiling—water. Remove when the soap melts. When it cools, you'll have a new bar of soap.

◆ Keep homemade ice packs in the freezer for the occasional sprain or aching muscle. To make a small ice pack, pour 1 cup Rite Aid isopropyl rubbing alcohol and 2 cups water into a quart-size GLAD Freezer Zipper Bag. Squeeze out air and seal. The mixture will remain slushy after time in the freezer, which is helpful for shaping around sprained knees or elbows. For large ice packs, use gallon-size bags and double the recipe.

◆ If you don't have an eyedropper handy, improvise with a drinking straw. Insert the straw into liquid and cover the open end with your finger; lift and use.

Maintenance and Projects

Conventional wisdom says that to maintain a house you need either the time (and expertise) to do the work yourself or the money to pay someone else to do it for you. These days, many people feel they don't have what it takes for either option. Sadly, a plastic grocery bag won't single-handedly overhaul your bathroom plumbing or double as a power drill. However, plastic bags (along with other plastic and paper goods) *can* help you improvise minor repairs, tend a garden even though your thumb is not so green, and reduce the pain of painting.

HANDYPERSON HINTS

Tips and Tools of the Trades

- Keep outdoor padlocks from freezing by covering them with sandwich-size GLAD Food Storage Zipper Bags. This will keep moisture from accumulating.

- Sandwich- or snack-size GLAD Food Storage Zipper Bags are great for storing small items such as screws, nuts, bolts, plastic fasteners, and hose washers at your workbench or in your toolbox.

- If your workshop is in the basement or cellar, store your matches in a snack- or sandwich-size GLAD Food Storage Zipper Bag to keep them dry.

- To prevent steel wool from rusting, store it in a GLAD Food Storage Zipper Bag. (Before storing, make sure the wool is completely dry.)

- To prevent the hassle of tangled string, wrap it on a Scott Towel core or other cardboard tube. Cut a small notch in each end of the tube. Anchor one end of the string in one notch, then wind the string tightly around the tube, securing the other end of the string in the other notch.

- To make it easier to feed a phone wire horizontally through a wall, drill a hole in the wall slightly bigger than the diameter of a drinking straw. Insert a straw and run the wire through it, then remove straw.

Caulk Talk and Shower Power

- Can't find the cap to a tube of caulk? Keep tube from drying out by closing it up in a GLAD Food Storage Zipper Bag.

- Caulking in a tight space? Attach a flexible drinking straw to the tube's nozzle; aim and squeeze.

- If a water faucet runs slowly, a clogged aerator may be the cause. Some newer styles cannot be taken apart, but before you run out and replace yours entirely, try filling a GLAD Food Storage Bag with Heinz Distilled White Vinegar and securing the bag around the spout with a rubber band. Leave in place overnight.

IN AND OUT OF THE GARAGE

- Seal the manuals and warranties for your grill, lawn mower, and other outdoor equipment in a gallon-size GLAD Freezer Zipper Bag. Hang in the garage.

- A damp, musty garage can be helped with this simple remedy: Add ½ inch ARM & HAMMER Baking Soda to the bottom of a paper grocery bag with handles; hang bag from the rafters. Change every 3 months.

Box o' Bags

Is your life, or at least your pantry, overrun with plastic grocery bags? Try this nifty storage idea. Squeeze the air from each bag, fold, and insert in an empty Kleenex facial tissue box. You won't believe how many bags can fit!

- If you don't have a garage and a snowstorm is coming, cover your car's side mirrors with GLAD Food Storage Zipper Bags held in place by clothespins or rubber bands. You won't have to scrape them later.

- Save yourself the trouble and discomfort that goes along with scraping snow and ice from your car's windshield. When a snowstorm is predicted, turn on the wipers, then stop them in mid-sweep; turn off the ignition. Split open a few paper grocery bags and secure them to the windshield using the wipers. When the snowstorm is over, pull off the paper—and the snow—before you start the engine.

- Prevent gasoline-scented hands at the pump by slipping a plastic grocery bag over each hand before you pump.

Mother of (Nearly) All Grocery Bags

The first recorded reference to paper grocery bags dates to 1630. Not until 1870, however, did Margaret Knight (1838–1914) invent an attachment for paper bag folding machines that created square-bottom bags. She founded the Eastern Paper Bag Company in Boston and continued her work, which resulted in more than 25 patents. At age 12 she made a safety device for textile looms; among her late inventions were improvements to clothing and shoe manufacturing, a numbering machine, a window frame and sash, and several devices for rotary engines.

◆ When you need to lubricate something that is out of reach, place a flexible drinking straw over the end of the spout of an oil can to extend its reach.

BRUSH UP ON PAINTING

◆ Make a paint smock from a GLAD trash bag. Cut holes for your arms and head. To make sleeves, cut off the ends of newspaper delivery bags and attach to the trash bag at the shoulders with Scotch Duct Tape. Plastic grocery bags or old, big sweat socks can protect your shoes.

◆ Keep some plastic grocery bags in your painting area. They may come in "handy" if you're a bit messy when the phone rings or someone's at the door.

◆ Protect light fixtures from errant paint splatters. Cover them with plastic grocery bags or GLAD trash bags, depending on their size. Be sure the light is off!

◆ Slip newspaper delivery bags on ceiling fan blades to protect them from paint drips.

- When you need to pause a painting project, instead of washing out your brush, tightly seal it in a GLAD Food Storage Zipper Bag. The paint won't dry out before you return. For breaks longer than a few days, store the brush in a GLAD Freezer Zipper Bag...and freeze it!

- Minimize the mess when spray-painting small items by placing them in an open paper grocery bag first.

- For a drip catcher that sticks with the job until it's done, attach a Dixie paper plate to your paint can using rubber cement or a few drops of Instant Krazy Glue.

- Using an electric drill and mixing attachment to stir paint can create a lot of splatter. To contain the mess, cover the paint can with a Dixie paper plate, then punch a hole in the center and insert the attachment.

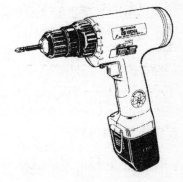

NATURE OF THE SITUATION

Gardening

- Store leftover seeds in small GLAD Food Storage Zipper Bags in a cool, dry place.

- Some seeds can only get off to a good start in cold and moisture. Put a Melitta Basket Coffee Filter in a pint- or quart-size GLAD Food Storage Zipper Bag; pour 3 tablespoons of water over the filter. Place seeds, evenly spaced, on the filter. Refrigerate the bag until the seeds sprout.

- Compost heaps (as well as earthworms) welcome brown 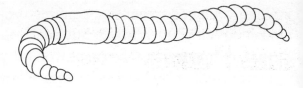 paper bags. Shred and dampen the bags, then mix in well so the pieces won't blow away when they dry.

- Transform cores from rolls of Scott Towels and Reynolds Wrap Aluminum Foil into mini seedling pots. Cut the cardboard tubes into pieces about 3 inches long. Wrap the outside (but not the ends) of each with aluminum foil to keep the wet cardboard from falling apart. Place the "pots," closely packed, in a waterproof tray or shallow pan. Fill each with seed-starting mix and plant seeds. When seedlings are ready, remove the foil and plant them in your garden—pots and all.

Pesky Pests

- To apply bug spray to your face without getting it in your eyes or mouth, toss a few Rite Aid cotton balls into a quart- or gallon-size GLAD Food Storage Zipper Bag. Spray in some bug spray, seal the bag, and shake it. Use the cotton balls to apply the bug spray.

- Flypaper will keep your family happy! Mix 1 cup Karo Corn Syrup (Light or Dark), 1 tablespoon Domino Brown Sugar, and 1 tablespoon Domino Demerara Washed Raw Cane Sugar; set aside. Cut a brown paper bag into 1-inch-wide strips. With a hole punch or small knife, make a hole near the top of each strip. Put a string through each hole. Brush the sweet concoction onto the strips, then hang them where flies hang out.

Creative Touches and Family Fun

Holiday traditions, arts and crafts, taking care of a pet, going on a long-awaited vacation—these are the things that create memories and nurture family joy.

These also, unfortunately, are the things that can cause nightmares and stir up family feuds. But help is nearby—it's probably already in your kitchen. Brown paper grocery bags, drinking straws, and simple sandwich bags can inspire enormous amounts of creativity and fun.

HINTS FOR THE HOLIDAYS

◆ Store the greeting cards you received this Christmas in a GLAD Food Storage Zipper Bag. Pull out the bag next November to create your next greeting card list, then cut up the cards to make decorative gift tags.

◆ The holiday has passed, and it's time to take down the decorative window clings. Store them in GLAD Food Storage Zipper Bags to keep them nice and neat. Place a bag flat on your work surface and lay a set of clings on the bottom inside wall, making sure each adheres completely and is not touching any other. Working up from the bottom of the bag, carefully push out air and seal the bag. (Works for gel and vinyl varieties.)

◆ Give yourself a present *now* for next year! To store a string of holiday lights, take a Scott Towel core (or

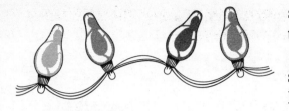

similar cardboard tube) and cut 1-inch vertical slits at each end. Insert the outlet plug end of the light string in one slit and tuck the plug inside the tube. Starting at that end, wind the cord carefully and evenly around the tube. Secure the other end of the cord in the slit at the other end of the tube.

CRAFTY THINKING

Kept in Stitches

♦ Why struggle to cram used sewing pattern pieces back into their original envelope? Fold the pieces, then store them and the envelope (front facing out) in a quart- or gallon-size GLAD Food Storage Zipper Bag.

♦ Prevent stains from a just-oiled sewing machine by stitching several rows on a Scott Towel or two before sewing fabric.

♦ Save fabric remnants in an old Scott Towel core or other cardboard tube. Cut an unused tube lengthwise, insert the rolled-up fabric, and close with rubber bands or transparent tape. On the tube, write information such as fabric type, color, yardage, and date.

♦ Store knitting needles in an old Scott Towel core. Cover one end with strips of transparent tape; pinch the other end closed and tape it securely with Scotch Duct Tape.

Slide the needles into the tube through the transparent tape, which will hold them in place.

Flowery Words

◆ Collect dried flowers and pinecones, and store them in a GLAD Food Storage Zipper Bag. Add McCormick Bay Leaves, Whole Cloves, and 1 Cinnamon Stick, plus a few drops of cinnamon essential oil. Keep the bag sealed for a few weeks, then place the potpourri in decorative bowls throughout your house.

◆ Dry flowers by placing them between 2 Scott Towels and inserting between the pages of a telephone book. Add weight by placing another telephone book or other heavy object on top. Let dry several weeks.

ACTIVITIES AND CRAFTS FOR CHILDREN

◆ To make a sun catcher, shave Crayola Crayons or colorful candle pieces onto a sheet of Reynolds Cut-Rite Wax Paper. Place another sheet on top, then put the whole set inside a paper grocery bag or between 2 pieces of cloth. Using a low setting, iron the "sandwich" until the shavings melt (try 10 seconds at first). Carefully peel bag or cloth off the wax paper. Let cool, then cut the wax paper art into a fun shape. Poke a hole in it and use ribbon to hang it by a window.

- Here's a project from yesteryear—creating place mats, bookmarks, book covers, or other decorative pieces. Arrange items such as colorful autumn leaves, flowers, or magazine pictures on a sheet of Reynolds Cut-Rite Wax Paper. Cover with another sheet. Put the whole stack inside a paper grocery bag or between 2 pieces of cloth. Iron on a low setting to melt the wax, creating a seal. Carefully remove the bag or cloth from the wax paper. Let cool, then cut to the shape and size you wish. If desired, use pinking shears to make interesting edges.

- Cut colored drinking straws into half-inch sections, and string the pieces on Reach dental floss to make colorful necklaces.

- Run the string of a pull toy through a drinking straw and knot it at the end. This will prevent tangling.

- Use a flexible drinking straw as a bubble blower. Cut one end on a diagonal and dip that end into bubble liquid. Have a child blow into the other end.

- Make your croquet wickets more visible on the lawn by running them through colorful, flexible drinking straws.

- Have your kids make their own kazoos. Cut 3 small holes, aligned vertically, in the middle of a Scott Towel core. Cover one end of the cardboard tube with Reynolds Cut-Rite Wax Paper, and use rubber bands to hold wax paper in place. Hum into the open end and cover 1, 2, or 3 holes with your fingers to change the pitch.

TRICKS FOR PETS AND PEOPLE

- You and your dog are hitting the trail. Before you hike, fill a quart- or gallon-size GLAD Food Storage Zipper Bag with water. Force out the air, and seal the bag. You'll have a portable water dish in your pack.

- When you give your pet a bath—and you don't really need one yourself just then—protect your clothes with a make-shift poncho. Simply cut holes for your arms and head in a GLAD trash bag.

- Keep a few old Scott Towel cores in the car. When your student gets in the car with a test or piece of artwork that's a keeper, roll the piece up and put it inside the core to protect it.

Fish Bowl Fun

Tissue paper or crepe paper (assorted colors)
Dixie paper plate
Elmer's Glue-All or Washable School Glue
Fish pictures from magazines
Scissors
GLAD Cling Wrap
Transparent tape
Hole punch
Yarn
Optional: fish-shape crackers, leaves, or shells

1. Rip up the tissue or crepe paper into small pieces. Glue to paper plate to make an underwater scene. Suggestions: blue on top for water, tan or yellow at bottom for sand, green for plants, and pink and orange for coral.

2. Glue fish pictures from magazines to the plate. If you like, also glue on crackers, leaves, and shells. Let dry.

3. Cover the whole plate with a piece of GLAD Cling Wrap. Tape in place on back of plate.

4. Punch a hole in center top of plate. Hang with yarn.

- Before you pass around those great new photos of your kitten, your children or grandchildren, or last week's trip, seal each one in its own sandwich-size GLAD Food Storage Zipper Bag. They'll be safe from smudges or spills.

- Help students keep track of school supplies: Punch 2 holes along the bottom edge of a quart-size GLAD Freezer Zipper Bag and place in a three-ring binder. Although this pencil pouch doesn't have unlimited capacity, it will hold a small supply of pencils, pens, erasers, paper clips, index cards, and/or Post-it Notes.

- Store and protect an item such as a diploma, a certificate, or a piece of your child's artwork by rolling the item up and inserting it into an empty Scott Towel core, gift wrap tube, or similar piece of cardboard packaging. Write pertinent information on the tube to identify its contents at a glance.

- Hamsters and other small pets love to run through, hide in, and chomp on cardboard cores from rolls of Scott Towels and other products. Replace the tubes when they look too ragged.

VACATION-SAVERS

- Store liquid toiletries in GLAD Food Storage Zipper Bags so they won't ruin clothes if they break or spill.

- Carry fresh diapers in a gallon-size GLAD Food Storage Zipper Bag. The bag can serve as a changing mat, then store dirty diapers until you get to a trash receptacle.

- Pack a child's suitcase using a gallon-size GLAD Food Storage Zipper Bag for each day of the trip. Put a complete outfit, including socks and underwear, into each bag. This makes dressing a snap and helps keep the suitcase tidy.

- Think ahead before you take a water ride—in a canoe, kayak, or any type of boat. Put your keys, cell phone, and other  small valuables in a quart- or gallon-size GLAD Food Storage Zipper Bag. Blow air into it and seal. The boat tips over... but the bag floats!

- When it's lunchtime at the beach, every hand is covered in sand. Think ahead and bring a gallon-size GLAD Food Storage Zipper Bag filled with a generous amount of Johnson's Baby Powder. Put both hands in the bag; remove and rub them together. The sand will just slip off.

- Store miscellaneous camping items (food, medicine, batteries, and so on) in individual GLAD Food Storage Zipper Bags to keep them dry and organized.

- Store salt, pepper, and other spices for a camp cookout in drinking straws. Fold over the end of a straw to seal it; secure with a small rubber band. Pour a spice into the straw, then fold over and secure the other end with another rubber band. Label each filled straw with a marking pen.

Trademark Information

Argo Corn Starch® is a registered trademark of the ACH Food Companies, Inc.

ARM & HAMMER® is a registered trademark of Church & Dwight Co., Inc.

Clabber Girl Baking Powder® is a registered trademark of Clabber Girl Corporation.

Clorox® is a registered trademark of The Clorox Company.

Crayola® is a registered trademark of Binney & Smith Properties, Inc.

Crisco® is a registered trademark of the J.M. Smucker Co.

Dixie® is a registered trademark of Fort James Operating Company.

Dole Crushed Pineapple® is a registered trademark of Dole Food Company, Inc.

Domino Sugar® is a registered trademark of Domino Foods, Inc.

GLAD® is a registered trademark of Union Carbide Corporation.

Heinz® is a registered trademark of H. J. Heinz Company.

Ivory® is a registered trademark of Procter & Gamble.

Karo® is a registered trademark of CPC International, Inc.

Kleenex® is a registered trademark of Kimberly-Clark Corporation.

Kraft® is a registered trademark of Kraft Holdings, Inc.

Krazy® is a registered trademark of Borden.

McCormick® is a registered trademark of McCormick & Company, Incorporated.

Melitta Basket Coffee Filter® is a registered trademark of the Melitta Group.

Morton Salt® is a registered trademark of Morton International, Inc.

O-Cel-O® is a registered trademark of 3M.

Parsons'® is a registered trademark of Church & Dwight Co., Inc.

Post-it® is a registered trademark of 3M.

Reynolds Cut-Rite® Wax Paper is a registered trademark of Reynolds Metals.

Reynolds Wrap® is a registered trademark of Reynolds Metals.

Scotch® is a registered trademark of 3M.

Scott Towels® is a registered trademark of Kimberly-Clark Worldwide, Inc.

20 Mule Team Borax® is a registered trademark of The Dial Corporation.